EVEN IN THIS

EVEN IN THIS

PEACE AND HEALING IN THE MIDST OF HARDSHIPS

Teresa Everett Horne

Diligence Publishing Company
Bloomfield, New Jersey

The Scripture in this book is from various versions of the Bible including, but not limited to the King James Version and the New International Version.

EVEN IN THIS

Copyright © 2018 Teresa Everett Horne
c/o Diligence Publishing Company
P.O. Box 2476
Bloomfield, New Jersey

All Rights Reserved

No part of this book may be reproduced in any form without the written permission from the author except for brief passages included in a review.

To contact Teresa Everett Horne to preach or speak at your church, organization, seminar or conference email:

divinepurpose08@yahoo.com

EVEN IN THIS

Printed in the United States

TABLE OF CONTENTS

INTRODUCTION 9
CHAPTER 1 11
Dee's Life And Upbringing 11
CHAPTER 2 15
Growing Up Years 15
CHAPTER 3 21
High School And College Experience 21
CHAPTER 4 25
Mother And Son Special Times 25
CHAPTER 5 29
Sibling Bonds 29
CHAPTER 6 33
Personal, But Not So Personal Experiences 33
CHAPTER 7 43
Greatest Heartaches 43
CHAPTER 8 53
Tips On Dealing With Mental Illness (Depression) 53
CHAPTER 9 59
A Cry For Help 59
CHAPTER 10 67
Tips On Dealing With Bereaved Families 67
CHAPTER 11 71
Facebook Posts 71
CHAPTER 12 77
Special Tributes 77

ABOUT THE AUTHOR 95
ORDER INFORMATION 97

SPECIAL THANKS

Special thanks to all our family, friends, and loved ones who embraced and loved on us during those difficult times and even now in our moments of healing.

I thank God for my husband, Gregory, who just holds me, cries with me, and listens to me whenever I need that extra strength. My baby girl, Alexus, who is so awesome and strong, both physically and spiritually; I thank you more than you'll ever know.

Casey Clark, I could never thank you enough for your support, encouragement, and the video of you singing the song *(You Are My Strength)* that helps me get through my days.

To all the churches, pastors, leaders, towns, cities and communities who prayed for and supported us, thank you.

Most of all, we thank God for His love, grace, mercy, strength, peace, and comfort. **Even in This**, God still gets all the glory!

INTRODUCTION

The title of my book, "**Even In This**" was released unto me through the Holy Spirit. The day after my son's (Dee) passing, I was in a very deep state of disbelief, denial, and not understanding the how's and why's of this happening. I had so many mixed emotions at this point and found myself with more questions than answers.

As I was crying out to God, the Holy Spirit spoke these words to me: "Even when you don't understand, trust me. **Even in this**, I'm going to get the glory." So, I had to trust God.

A couple of days later, my husband and I got in contact with Pastor Tony Hinton whom Dee had requested to do his eulogy, and he told us that he had heard the Lord say, "**Even in This**."

The following day, Prophetess Felicia Farmer Winstead came along and prophesied to me that God wanted a book to be published and she even gave me the title of the book, "**Even in This**."

God confirmed Himself repeatedly and this became and is our daily declaration: "**Even in This,**" God gets the glory. Many of our friends and family members continue the saying: "**Even in This**." At the homegoing service, "**Even in This**" was sung on Dee's behalf.

CHAPTER 1

Dee's Life And Upbringing

At the tender age of 16, I gave birth to my son Demetrius Devon Everett on December 2, 1980. Oh, what an intense and excruciating birth it was; twenty-four long hours of labor which resulted in me having a C-section.

Dee was a healthy bouncing boy weighing in at 9 pounds, 14 ounces, and 20 inches long. I knew right then that I had a unique young man to look forward to.

With the help of my loving family and friends, I was able to complete high school, graduate, and work a fulltime job. I was determined to not add to the already "labeled" status of being dependent on government assistance.

Although many thought that I should have gone to college, I knew in my heart that college at that point in my life was not for me, so I continued to work and raise my son. While I was still living at home, my Mom and stepfather cared for my son while I worked. God had blessed my Mom and stepfather with a son whom we called "Papa." My son Dee and Papa grew up together and became "partners in crime." They had some amazing times together as they were growing up. They stayed in "trouble" as we called it. One followed the other being mischievous and spontaneous.

As the years continued to move forward, these two little "rascals" became best friends. It was strange to see one of them and not the other. This was because they were always together and "into something." They played together, got into "trouble" together, laughed together, and even cried together when they got punished for doing something they had no business doing. They were like "peanut butter and jelly" – inseparable. They often walked to the local store and spent all their little "hard earned" money on candy and cookies.

I remember a time when they walked a couple of blocks to a local small restaurant called Kearney's BBQ, and they would order food knowing they had little to no money. Papa told the worker that his Dad was going to come and pay for the food. Somehow, they ended up with the food, but I'm not sure if the food was ever paid for. You know what I mean? LOL.

These two guys kept something going all the time. There was never a dull moment with them around. It was a blessing seeing the two of them growing up together. They were a hot mess at times, but at the end of the day, they were still the best of buddies.

At the ages of 8 and 10, the two of them became separated when I got married in 1988 and moved out on my own; and even that did not separate the two for long. I would often bring them together on weekends for some more enjoyable and fun moments. They would have fun at the swimming pool, the movies, or just enjoying each other's company. When the weekend was about over, they knew it was time to say, "See you later man."

And yes, they acted like two old men. They were the best of buddies.

CHAPTER 2

Growing Up Years

As the years went by, I began to see some unique characteristics in my baby boy. He was very jovial and would keep people laughing.

He would always make those around him smile and have fun even when the times didn't permit laughter and fun.

I considered him to be somewhat of a humorous child but still quiet and laid back. He had certain people who he really interacted with.

Yes, even as a child he was unique and peculiar. It was as if his little mind was already set and programmed as to what he liked and disliked in life. He was set in his own ways and these ways lingered on into his teenage years. As a teenager, he still possessed that jovial spirit. He kept his friends and family laughing and joking. At family gatherings, Dee was the comedian, and everyone just loved that rascal. At Thanksgiving and Christmas gatherings, Dee would just walk, talk, and eat, walk, talk, and eat while picking on folk, all at the same time. He could really eat too.

He was known for picking on his Great Auntie Gert and his favorite Auntie Jessica (Jet). Man, he gave them a run for their money, but they loved him, and he loved them.

Now, while he was at my Mom's house, they had something going on in that house. Dee would jump on her bed and lay like he was a baby and all she would say was, "Ball Ball, you better get off of my bed."

Oh, and by the way, she called him "Ball Ball." My Mom had that rascal so spoiled rotten to the point that she would pick the bones out of his fish before he would eat it. She didn't like for anyone to mess with her "Ball Ball."

One Saturday afternoon while at my house, my friends and I were outside cooking on the grill and Dee was having a rough day. It was a hot day outside, and I guess he had something on his mind. I had asked him to help me move the grill into a shady area, and his response to me was, "Come on now Ma. I'm already HOT, TIRED, and FRUSTRATED."

Man, if we didn't have a good ole laughing and crying time at that child. Now, what did he know about being "HOT, TIRED, and FRUSTRATED?"

Dee always kept people laughing. At school he was the same way. He had his classmates and even the teachers laughing. The classroom was full of excitement and laughter. I remember him talking about feeding the frogs flies at school and how one of the teachers would cough constantly while trying to teach. Now, you know his classmates got a good laugh out of that. The teachers would call me about once a week talking about how Dee had the class laughing, but they must have loved his jovial behavior because all they did as far as punishment was to have him sit underneath a large desk/table, or he had to write "I will listen and not cause trouble" 100 times.

Yes, I remember this stuff because Dee was a jovial and lovable young man who loved to keep people smiling and happy. If he saw or heard of someone not feeling well, Dee would go to them and before he left them, they were laughing and had a smile on their face. God truly blessed him with that special and unique gift.

CHAPTER 3

High School And College Experience

Throughout his high school days, the same pattern of uniqueness continued. This guy was so funny, and the jokes and laughter intensified. Although he had this jovial behavior, his grades were not affected. He did well and even found laughter in his schoolwork.

I remember him asking one teacher if he could do a makeup test "open book." The teacher asked him why she should allow him that privilege when everyone else didn't have it, and his response was; "I heard that everyone else failed the test, so don't you want somebody to pass?"

Dee loved his classmates and teachers. He enjoyed attending all the athletic activities in high school, however he only participated in wrestling for which he won several awards and medals. High school was an era of growth and development for Dee in many areas. His friends were important to him and some of them became a part of our family. Some of his friends spent time with him at our home, and I treated them as my own.

He began to start looking and thinking more like an adult with envisions of his future. Physically, he was growing rapidly; muscular and

HIGH SCHOOL AND COLLEGE EXPERIENCE

in strength, and mentally he began to take life situations and decisions more seriously.

High school was a time of much laughter and fun for Dee, but also a time of amazing change and growth. God blessed him to graduate from high school, but he had not fully made up his mind about furthering his education, so he gained employment before deciding to attend North Carolina Central University in Durham, North Carolina. He attended there for a while and came to the conclusion that he wasn't "college material." He came back home and gained full-time employment.

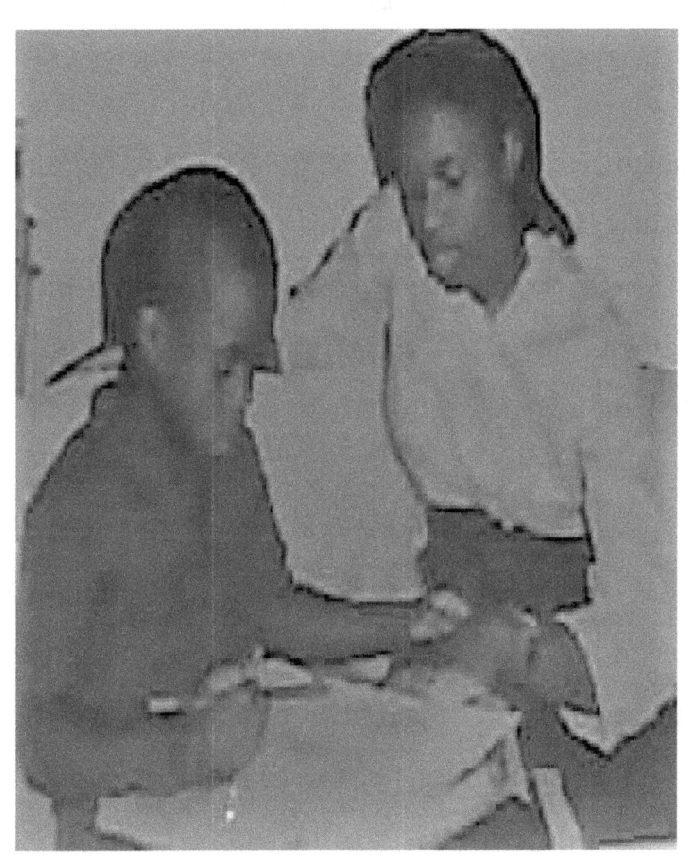

CHAPTER 4

Mother And Son Special Times

I had become a single mom during Dee's sophomore year. As a result, he had become very caring, supportive, and protective of me.

Whatever I needed or even wanted, he made sure I got it. He helped around the house while maintaining his job.

The growth and development I saw in him in high school was being manifested in his life. We became the best of friends, and we enjoyed life and each other.

Even at this point in our lives, Dee was still jovial and kept people laughing and smiling on the job and at home. That was just a God-given gift that he was destined to fulfill.

A few years later, I began to socialize a lot more than I had been. I figured that I had done an excellent job in raising him and that now it was time for me to enjoy my life in a different way. I began to date and "thought" that I was in love. Sometime further into the relationship, I found myself pregnant. This was such a "shocker" to me, but God gave me peace and His forgiveness even in this state.

When we decided to tell Dee, I thought he would be "shocked" but he picked at me and was the first one to spread the news. He took the ultrasounds everywhere he went and showed them to everybody. He thought this was so funny while I was still somewhat in denial.

Even in the laughing and joking times, he still made sure I was well taken care of. Dee loved his "Momma" and I loved him too. As my due date was getting closer, Dee made sure he stayed around the house. He was excited, and he even helped buy things for the baby.

Well, my due date arrived, and God blessed us with a healthy, bouncing, beautiful baby girl, Alexus.

CHAPTER 5

Sibling Bonds

Alexus stole Dee's heart from day one of her birth, and she became his pride and joy. Anything I needed done, Dee was right there. He helped me with her like she was his very own child.

Every birthday, he gave her a party. Every Christmas, he bought her gifts of all kinds. He even helped her in her walking stages. When she would fall, he was right there to pick her up. When she finally started walking well, Dee and Alexus would have a ball.

When his friends would come over to the house, he would be very protective of her. He watched her every move, whether she was awake or asleep.

Dee suffered with asthma and so the doctor had recommended that I do whatever it took to make him comfortable during the attacks. So, through trial and error, we discovered that sleeping on an air mattress on the floor, which was better than sleeping on a bed, worked for him. As he slept on the mattress on the floor, Alexus would stay in his room right beside him. They would play and have fun, and he enjoyed it just as much as Alexus did.

After he would get off work, he would find somewhere to take her. Sometimes he would take her riding out to the mall, the park, and he would even take her to the basketball games at the high school. He would have her diaper bag all packed and everything, and he would always have one of his female friends to help him with her at the games when needed.

People had begun to question him about whether Alexus was his baby, and you know he would get a good laugh out of that. Everywhere he went, basically, he took her with him, and I was grateful for the help.

As the years continued to move forward and Alexus was getting older, Dee continued to show brotherly love towards her. As she went into her school days, on his days off from work, he would help me get her dressed and watch her get on the bus as I was heading off to work. He made sure that on his days off he was home when she got off the school bus.

Dee took very good care of his baby sister while he lived with us. He eventually moved out, and it was then just Alexus and me. Even that move didn't stop him from spending time with us, but it wasn't like it used to be. I understood because he was getting older, and he wanted to enjoy his life as well. He would call every day and come by when he wasn't working or busy.

CHAPTER 6

Personal, But Not So Personal Experiences

Now at this time, Dee was much older, becoming more sociable, and joining some of his peers in different life activities; some good and some not so good. It was at this point in his life that I truly recognized the call of God upon his life. Now mind you, he had accepted Jesus as his personal Lord and Savior years ago. There were a few times when life got the best of him, and it caused him to have to call on God to bring him out of certain things.

One time I can remember that Dee was going through a situation, and he truly cried out to God for deliverance. He called me early one morning crying. I asked him what was wrong, and he said, "Ma, I just need you to pray me through this."

So, I began to pray with him, and he cried out profusely unto the Lord even the more. He cried and prayed, cried and prayed, and then he began to speak in his "heavenly" language. Then he turned around and interpreted it.

We continued in prayer until God released his breakthrough, and he was delivered early that Sunday morning. I knew from that point forward that he was called by God, but he was fighting the call.

Years went by, and Dee continued to run from the calling upon his life. He found himself in situations that only God continued to bring him through time after time.

Some of the people he found himself connected with were not in his best interest, and he recognized it but was unwilling to disconnect.

Once again, he found himself involved in ungodly relationships and activities. Even though he had accepted Jesus as his Lord and personal Savior, he still dealt with strongholds that kept him in dark situations.

As a concerned parent, I did all I could and all that he would allow me to do to steer him in the ways of God according to Proverbs 22:6, *"Train up a child in the way he should go: and when he is old, he will not depart from it."*

Even in spite of my teachings, he chose to live his life the way he wanted, so I just prayed and continued to check on him daily. At this point of his life he was living with my Mom, whom he called "Ma."

Years passed by and Dee was set in his own ways, growing up into his manhood stage, and living his life as such. At this stage of his life, he was traveling and enjoying life while continuing to work.

I didn't really know much about his friends and social life at this time because he was a "grown" young man. No young person at this stage of life tells his or her parents their "business." They just enjoy life to the fullest, and that's what Dee did at this point. We began to become more distant in our relationship, but yes, we did stay in contact quite often, and that was fine with me because I understood that he had a life to live. I was just happy to even be a part of his life and see him doing well. He even remained in contact with his sister. He loved this young girl, and she still loved him too.

Now, I'm seeing my son doing well and loving life, so I decided that it was time for me to experience a new life. At this point, I rarely heard from Dee because he was in his own world, enjoying his life with his "friends." The phone calls and the text messages had all stopped, but my prayers for him never did. The young man I once was so close to had become like a total stranger to my daughter and myself, but the Lord would always have me in prayer covering him.

So now our relationship had gone from great to not so great, but still Alexus and I loved him. When we'd have family gatherings at my Mom's house, Dee would always overlook Alexus and me, but we continued to fellowship with the family.

During this period, I prayed and asked God what had we done so bad that would have caused the relationship to be so dysfunctional, and the Lord let me know that it wasn't anything Alexus or I had done; but it was Dee's own personal reasons and that he had to deal with life in a better way. I constantly prayed for my son, but the enemy had consumed his mind so intensely to the point wherein he thought that I was his enemy.

For years Dee treated me as if I wasn't his mother, but I continued to pray for him. At times, I began to blame myself because people were looking at me as if I had done something drastic to my own child. I finally came to the conclusion that I was ready to move on with my life and just be happy; for I had done about all I could do to rebuild the relationship.

So, I prayed "this" time and asked God for my husband. While I was preparing for my husband, God was working on me to be the wife that I needed to be. It was about two years before the Lord sent my husband. When we officially met, we both knew that God was in the midst, so we started dating and were married months later. Oh, how I wanted to tell Dee about my new life, but our relationship was so "messed" up, and I knew he wouldn't want to be a part of my new life, so I just began to enjoy the journey that God had blessed me with.

As time passed by, my husband and I tried reaching out to Dee, but he was angry and bitter because I had gotten married. Several times I asked him why he was so angry and bitter, and he accused me of getting married unbeknownst to him. Mind you now, I had tried many times to reach out to him, but he was in his own little world and doing what made him happy.

Dee was selfish and stubborn at times. He wanted things to be his way. He didn't mind expressing his feelings either, and when he did, people recognized his actions. So now at this point in his life, he was filled with all kinds of negative emotions and strongholds, and our relationship was for sure now "shot." My husband and I did all we could to reach out to him, but he refused anything from us. My husband loved Dee as his own biological son and always asked had I heard from or seen him. When we'd go out for dinner sometimes, we'd want to bring Dee something back, but knew he wouldn't accept it.

We dealt with these types of issues for a few years, but we still believed that God would restore the relationship. We didn't know how or when He would do it, but we knew that He would do it for us, so we kept on praying for Dee.

As time went by, Dee began to slow down a little. He had gotten another job and seemed to be happy and doing well. At this point, Dee had begun to simplify his life. He went to work and spent a lot of his time at home with his Granny. He loved when his "favorite" Auntie Jessica came home from Maryland. She spoiled him slam rotten and oh, how he did love that. He also loved when his favorite cousin/sister, Brittany and her daughter Kendall came home. He loved when we had family gatherings at "Granny's house." He kept the life in the house going strong with his jokes and constant eating. This dude could really eat and didn't gain a pound more. He'd have folk laughing so hard that they'd be crying. He was a jokester indeed and everybody loved him. He loved every restaurant that sold food...LOL.

He loved social media, and he communicated a lot through the various sites. The people on the different sites loved him and his daily postings. He shared from the heart, and he made people laugh with certain posts. Some of his posts shared personal feelings of his, and that's how I really began to see some of the struggles he was facing. When I recognized the struggles and strongholds, I began to reach out more, but he refused to open up to me, so all I could do was pray a little harder and trust God to intervene.

Over a period of time, our relationship had gotten a little better in between time. We were talking and texting each other, not every day, but that did make me feel a little better because I loved my son, and I knew he loved me. Sometimes the enemy will cause us to be distracted and cause division. That's exactly what happened, but I began to see God restoring our relationship. It wasn't quite where I wanted it to be, but I was pleased at where we had gotten to. It didn't stop me from praying and loving him. As a matter of fact, I prayed even the more for him. He'd started to open up a little more on social media and through text messages, which was fine with me. Something was better than nothing at this point. When I'd go visit my Mom, either he was gone or in his room asleep, so I didn't get to see him that often. He was still working, so I figured he was doing okay.

CHAPTER 7

Greatest Heartaches

On November 5, 2017, Dee called and asked me to meet him at the hospital because he wasn't feeling well. Hurriedly, my husband, my daughter and I rushed to the hospital.

Dee was very ill and was admitted into the hospital. He stayed there a week and was released on that Friday, only to return early on Monday morning. In my heart, I believed he wanted to be released on that Friday so that he could spend time with his Granny. My baby was very weak and ill. He was seen by the ER doctors and staff for about seven hours before being placed in a room. His diagnosis was very heartbreaking, but my family and others were interceding on his behalf. **#EvenInThis**, we continued to trust God for a miracle.

Every day for three consecutive weeks, I was at his bedside praying and believing God for a miracle. During his weeks in the hospital, Dee still had that sense of joking and laughter. He had the doctors and the nurses laughing. Even in his condition, I saw God restoring our relationship. That was part of my daily prayer. He wanted me to sit on his bed, and he would rub my hands, pinch my legs, and joke.

One day, he wanted some Little Debbie's Christmas tree cakes, so we got him some, and the rascal tore them up. Then he wanted something from the cafeteria. We got him a sub, chips, a fruit cup, and a drink. This child was still eating, which was a good thing. After eating, he'd get him a nap. My husband and I would stay right there until he woke up. When he would wake up, he'd start joking again about anything. I was so loving our bonding even in those moments.

He was on a lot of medication during this stay. Some of the meds made him tired and sleepy, but he kept on trying to remain positive. He would ask me to get Pandora on his phone, and he would listen to Gospel music. He would sing, wave his hands. and just praise and worship God. Every day he would sing, "There's not a friend like the lowly Jesus. No not one. No not one." As he would sing, his hands would be waving. He had this smile on his face that was like no other.

As I watched Dee praising and worshipping God, it was as if he and God had already had some conversations about his situation. He was at peace while he yet continued to laugh and make jokes with us.

Despite all the tests and procedures that he was undergoing, he did not complain. He was still polite and respectful towards the doctors, nurses and other staff members. He knew every staff member by name, and they treated him well. One day one of the nurses told him how respectful he was, and he pointed to me and told the nurse, "I get it from that woman right there. My Momma."

That made me so proud of him for making that kind of reference of me. At this moment, **#EvenInThis**, I was seeing the child that I had birthed and raised. I saw the child that I wished had been more open with me concerning the things he was going through and maybe, just maybe, I could have helped him. But at this point, all that I could do to help him, I had done it to the best of my ability. He was in God's hands and I knew that God's will would be done.

Days went by and Dee was getting weaker, but **#EvenInThis**, he continued to praise God. He continued to laugh and joke, and he kept something going. Because of all the medication he was on and the constant procedures he had to go through, he really was exhausted and didn't want a lot of visitors, but he reached out to family and friends while in the hospital. He had requested that Granny call him every night, and that request was fulfilled. He waited patiently and with great expectation of seeing his "favorite" Auntie. When she came, I guess he thought he had a billion dollars. The smile on his face extended from "here to there." He was glad to see her. She spent the weekend with him. I can only imagine what they talked about, but I believe they were able to personally share.

While we were with him on that Saturday night, Dee gave everyone a scare. He was very, very ill, so my sister called and told us to get there ASAP. My husband, daughter, and I rushed back to the hospital, and after talking with the doctors, learned that they would be moving him to the Critical Care Unit. We all exchanged hugs, kisses, and "I love you's" before they moved him. At this point, all we could do was continue praying that God's will be done. It was hard, but we had to trust God **#EvenInThis.**

Days went by and things got a little "rougher" but the prayers were still going up, and we kept the faith that God's will would be done. We knew that Dee was in God's hands, but it was still hard to see your own this way.

Well, it was November 22, 2017 around noon time, and the doctors called me and gave me an update. My husband, daughter, and I went back to the hospital to meet with the hospital staff. We contacted relatives and friends that my son had requested, and they came to the hospital as well. The doctors gave us the full update, and I had to make a decision that I never thought I'd have to make in my life, but I remembered that one conversation I had with my son that included his wishes. It was hard to do, but I promised him that I would carry out his wishes so that's what I did.

The prayers never stopped, **#EvenInThis**. The family and friends began to arrive and embrace each other while taking turns going in and visiting him. We sang, cried, hugged on him, and loved on him. Around six-thirty that evening, the Lord called him home to be with Him. He looked at peace and even in all that he went through, there was a supernatural transformation upon his body. Dee looked really, really handsome in the Lord. It was difficult realizing that he was no longer with us but comforting just to know that He was now in no more physical or emotional pain. He was at peace with the Lord now.

And so, as each day goes by, it is those memories that cross my mind every now and then. Some days are better than others but **#EvenInThis**, I give God the glory. I think about how Dee kept people laughing, how he did mischievous pranks, how he rode by places hollering and waving at everybody, how he loved to eat, how he expressed wanting to be a dog catcher (lol) when he grew up, and most of all how he loved God and his family.

Dee was a fun loving and caring person, especially towards children. He loved children and would buy school supplies for the children as part of his annual "Back To School" project. If he could help anyone, he did. He would help the homeless with food. He loved to visit the nursing facilities and make the residents laugh. I remember one of the residents asking Dee to bring her some nail polish. Dee got some orange nail polish, and it made her day.

Dee was such an awesome young man, and I pray that we all that knew him remember him as such in our daily lives. I believe that if we would remember the good times of fun and laughter, God will give us that peace to move forward and just know that he is with God, and if we live according to the Word of God, we will one day see him again. Now, ain't that Good News? Again, I want to say to my family, thank you all for all acts of kindness shown towards us; then and even now. We love you all.

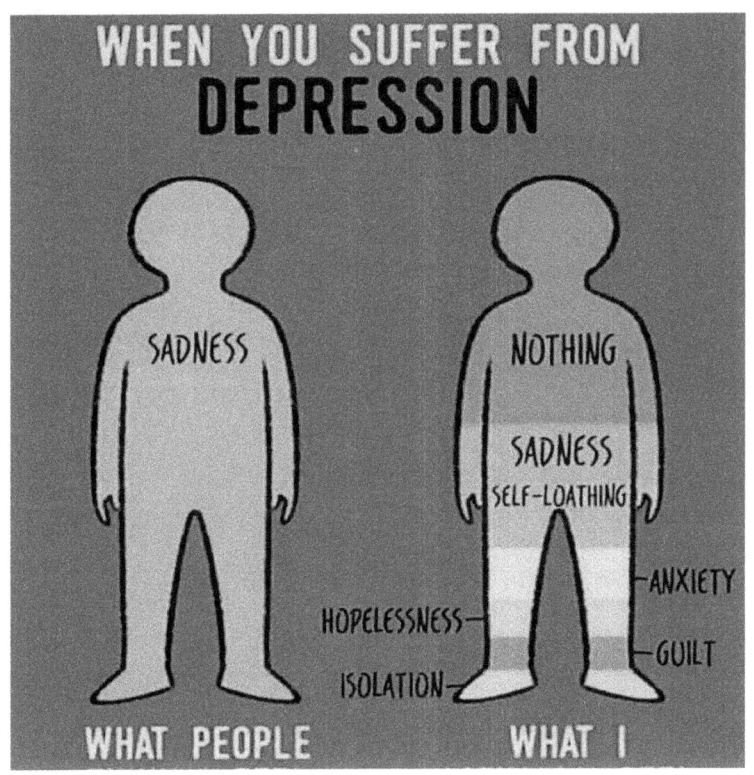

CHAPTER 8

Tips On Dealing With Mental Illness (Depression)

According to the American Psychiatric Association, Depression (major depressive disorder) is a common and serious medical illness that negatively affects how you feel, the way you think and how you act. Fortunately, it is also treatable. Depression causes feelings of sadness and/or a loss of interest in activities once enjoyed. It can lead to a variety of emotional and physical problems and can decrease a person's ability to function at work and at home.

Depression symptoms can vary from mild to severe and can include:

- Feeling sad or having a depressed mood.
- Loss of interest or pleasure in activities once enjoyed.
- Changes in appetite – weight loss or gain unrelated to dieting.
- Loss of energy or increased fatigue.
- Feeling worthless or guilty.
- Thoughts of death or suicide.
- Difficulty thinking, concentrating or making decisions.

(Source: www.psychiatry.org)

TIPS ON DEALING WITH MENTAL ILLNESS (DEPRESSION)

Depression is not just a feeling of "being sad" and not being able to "snap out of it." It's a medical condition that can and should be treated. The first step in dealing with mental illness (depression) is recognizing it and seeking effective treatment with a health care provider or even a spiritual leader about how you feel.

Depression and reaching out does not mean that there is a weakness, but rather that you are strong and desire help. Don't be ashamed or allow pride to hinder you from seeking help. Always try and get early treatment and care. Don't wait.

When dealing with mental illness (depression):

1) Surround yourself with positive people, including family, friends and loved ones, who can encourage and strengthen you.
2) Follow the care plan that professionals put in place for you.
3) Set small goals for getting better.

4) Pace yourself for getting better.
5) Do positive things that make you feel good, such as getting involved in social activities in your local community, finding a hobby or sport to explore, or just going out with friends.
6) Get proper rest.
7) Maintain good sleeping habits.
8) Eat healthy.

Don't allow the stigma of being "weak" to be used as an embarrassment or an excuse for not getting treatment. This has been seen as a huge issue, especially among Black males. They can sometimes feel "less than" a man when they seek help. Get help if you need it. It's okay. Other people are in need of your life and depending on you.

Don't allow the devil to make you feel that you don't need help or that you don't matter. It's his job to kill, steal, and destroy life, but our God is the Giver of abundant life. Receive that abundant life of treatment because God has purpose and destiny for your life. There is greatness in you.

Also, just know that you are not alone in this situation. First and foremost, for believers in Jesus Christ, always know that God is with you **#Eveninthis** situation. Remember that He will never leave nor forsake you. He will see you through, giving you instructions on how to handle everyday situations.

Get the available help and treatment, and fulfill your Kingdom assignment. Your life matters!!!

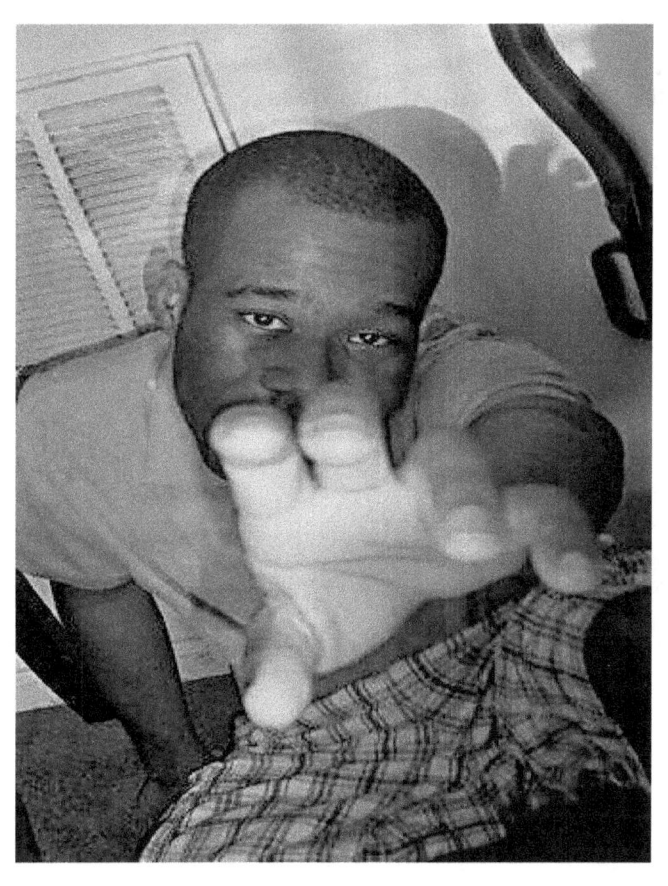

CHAPTER 9

A Cry For Help

During his life, my son was dealing with depression but refused to get help. He felt that he had no one to talk to that would understand him. Many times, I would talk with him, and I always prayed for him. He would ask me to never share with anyone what he was going through.

It truly hurt me to know that he was going through this and not wanting any help because he didn't trust people. I would often ask him to even go out of town for help, assuring him that I would take him there for appointments. I did it for a while, but he refused to continue the visits.

I did all I could do or rather all that he would allow me to do. I even reached out to clergy in whom I knew he thought highly of asking them to talk with him, but I'm not sure if they did or not. I didn't ever get any feedback from anyone. I spent countless hours in prayer for him and even had others praying on his behalf. He was just determined that he would be alright, and I could not make him (as an adult) receive treatment. So, I just prayed and showed him motherly love. I did all that he would allow me to do.

A CRY FOR HELP

The depression stronghold had a tight grip on him, and he began to shut me out of his life. He had stopped acknowledging me as his mother, and he stopped calling and messaging me. There were no more birthday gifts, Mother's Day gifts, or Christmas gifts. I had to deal with this hurt and pain as a mother who loved her child.

As this was taking place, to my knowledge, no one even addressed the issue with him. There were people who asked me why Dee treated me that way and my response to them was to pray for him. There were people who saw the mistreatment on his part, and they never said anything. So, I felt that they were giving him the okay to continue his behavior towards me. Many days and nights, I cried about this. I would ask God to give me strength and to heal my child of all the hurt he was going through.

Through much prayer and fasting, the Lord revealed to me that my son was going through a lot of struggles in life and felt that he had no one that he could really confide in. During this time, the Lord gave me instructions on how to go through this time with my son, and it didn't include sharing with everyone. He had me to share with certain people, so I did just that. Even after sharing with them and them trying to help, my son became even more withdrawn and angry. He was determined that he could fight these demons on his own. He didn't want anybody's help. So, after following the instructions of God, I just continued to ask those whom I had shared with to continue in prayer and fasting on his behalf.

This was such a painful and hurtful time of my life. I couldn't share with everyone because some things just couldn't and can't be shared, and Dee didn't want anyone in his "business." **#EvenInThis**, I continued to pray, fast, and give it to the Lord. It was too much for me to handle.

The Lord had given Dee a Word that if he did certain things, He (God) would heal, deliver, and set him free, but he chose to continue to walk in rebellion. This demon of depression had a tight grip on him, and he refused to allow anyone, even God, to step in and allow deliverance and healing to take place.

I want to encourage those who may be experiencing something in your lives that seems hard to handle, and you feel that you just can't make it or see your way out. I want you to know that there is hope. There is a way out, and His name is Jesus. Nothing is too hard for Almighty God. He is always with us and He cares for you. So whatever struggle, sickness, addiction, or hardship that you may be facing right now, just know that we serve an awesome and amazing God. He is our Peace in our going through. He is our Comforter late in the midnight hour. He is our Provider in our time of need. He is our Way Maker when there seems to be no way. He is our Joy, for the joy of the Lord is our strength. He is a Miracle

Worker when all else has failed. He is the True and Living God, and He loves us.

So, no matter what challenges are before you, just remember that Jesus is the answer. Trust Him to see you through life's trials and tribulations.

Proverbs 3:5 and 6 declares unto us that we are to *"Trust in the Lord with all thine heart; and lean not unto thine own understanding. In all thy ways acknowledge him, and he shall direct thy paths."* When we trust God, He gives us that peace which surpasses all understanding and gives us comfort in our going through.

Don't allow the things that you face to cause you to miss out on the abundant life that God has for you. Don't give the devil authority and access over your life. Pray and ask God for someone to confide in. Don't try to handle difficult life issues alone. When things are too big for us, they are just right for our big God.

Now, if you're reading this book and you have not accepted Jesus as Lord and personal Savior in your life, I strongly urge you to make that important decision today. It will not only save, deliver, and set you free, but it will help you build a strong and loving relationship with Almighty God. You'll be able to call upon His Name, and He will be with you to help in overcoming life's trials and tribulations. So, if you want to become a born-again believer of Almighty God, repeat this sinner's prayer, and after that, pray and ask God to lead you to a Bible-believing church that can help you in your spiritual growth and development.

"Dear God, I know that I am a sinner and there's nothing that I can do to bring salvation unto myself. I confess all my sins unto You because I want and need You in my life. I believe that You died for my sins on the cross. I believe that You were raised from the dead with all power in Your hands. As best I

know how, I trust You and I thank You for acceptingme. Now Lord, thank You for the assurance that You will be with me through every deep valley in my life. Thank You for hearing and answering my prayer. In Jesus' name. Amen."

Just a word of wisdom: It's not the prayer that saves us, but it's the repentance and faith behind the prayer that gives us a hold of salvation.

***Lord, thank You for every person who has purchased this book. May the blessings of You continue to richly bless them and their families. I thank You for allowing them to be a part of my son Dee's life; for he is at rest and peace now in You. In Jesus' name. Amen. ***

CHAPTER 10

Tips On Dealing With Bereaved Families

Having recently gone through the loss of a loved one, I'd like to share some things that can help families experiencing bereavement now or in the future.

1. Respect the families' wishes in every way possible.
2. Don't make the statement of "If there's anything I can do, let me know." If you're going to do something, just do it. We know somewhat the things needed.
3. Don't just bombard the families during the week of the loss and never show up the days, weeks, and months later. It's afterwards that they will need the support, prayers, and encouragement.
4. Don't talk so much, but pray more. Too much talking unnecessarily is not needed; especially at this time.
5. Respect families as they grieve and how they grieve. Everybody is different even in this process.
6. Love on these families because it could be the other way.

7. It's disrespectful to ask what happened to the deceased. Just know that they're no longer with us.

I have just shared a few pointers that could help families transition better during the bereavement, grief, and healing process. We need to be more sympathetic, caring, and compassionate towards others.

CHAPTER 11

Facebook Posts

- To those who have loved ones gone on, when the phone calls, text messages, and visits cease, the doorbell stops ringing, and the cards are no more, God's Word declares that He will never leave nor forsake us. He will be with us until the end of the world. So #EVENINTHIS, we're never alone. Be encouraged and strengthened in the Lord today and every day.

- I don't plan on making posts every day of the month that my brother passed away, but in honor of it being one month since he has passed away, I want to share with y'all the very last memory I shared/experienced with Dee. On November 21, 2017 (the day before he transitioned) it was just my brother and I in his room. After rubbing and holding his hand, I started singing *"You Are My Strength"* to him. I sang for about 10 minutes. Let me remind y'all, during this time my brother couldn't speak, interact with you, or anything like that. He was just lying there...fighting. However, after a few minutes of me singing, I saw him raise his left arm. Now I'm going to be honest. It did catch me off guard. I wasn't expecting that at all. Secondly, he shouldn't have been able to do that in the condition that he was in. So, it really did catch me off guard. But anyways, I kept on singing, and after a while Dee raised the same arm two more times and then lifted his head and slid it over. It really scared me then. 😢😨 I was looking for someone to call, just to make sure everything was okay...because I really didn't know what was going on. But on the inside, I honestly believe my brother did all of that to let me know that he was alright and that he could hear me. I truly believe that. Dee gave me a sign that even in his fighting, he was alright. That was the very last memory I had with him until his transition. To be honest, that's one of the only things that's really holding me up.

That, the prayers of others, and the help of the Holy Spirit. Even when I was singing that song, I believe the Holy Spirit gave my brother the strength to raise his arm three different times. I believe it was the Holy Spirit that gave my brother the strength to lift his head. And I also believe that the strength the Holy Spirit gave my brother is the same strength He has given me to endure the loss of my brother. I have experienced the loss of some very close family members and friends, but this is a whole different type of death. It still doesn't seem real. I just don't believe it should've gone the way it did. But **#EvenInThis** God is still good. He's still worthy to be praised. And I know that one day I will see my brother again. Not because of the good I have done. Not because of what I have or because of who I am... but because my SOUL is right with God, I have given my life to

God, and I have a personal relationship with Him. If we want to see our loved ones that have made it into Heaven, I suggest that we ALL have our SOULS right with God. Our good deeds & personalities aren't going to get us into Heaven. God looks at our SOULS. So **#EvenInThis** I pray that whoever is reading this post will make sure your SOUL is right with God. Make sure you have a personal relationship with God. Make sure, that you know that you know, that if you would die today, your SOUL will be right with God and Heaven would be your home. God bless you all...

#EvenInThis 🙏

CHAPTER 12

Special Tributes

Tribute #1

As I attempt to express my thoughts and feelings of gratitude towards my brother, I begin to get emotional and teary eyed. I never thought in a million years I would have to give a special tribute about my brother in this form.

Demetrius was my first oldest sibling and my oldest brother. I looked up to him in so many ways. He was the very first male that made sure I was well protected. I remember when I was just a little baby, he would take me to his school's sports events. Everybody thought he had a baby. When you saw Dee, you saw me. Although I was his little sister, the love he had for me would make you believe I was his own.

One of the many memories I remember sharing with him while being a little girl, was him picking me up from Hammond's Head Start. Once I got in my car seat, I saw a McDonald's kid's meal sitting to the side waiting for me. Boy was I happy! One thing Dee and I had in common was that we both loved to eat. No matter what the situation may be, we always had room to eat. We would continue eating even after we were full. Our favorite hashtag was #FoodIsBae. Food meant so much to us. It was one of our happy places. I believe that is one of the many reasons why we had such a great bond. The next food adventure date we went on was at IHOP. IHOP was my favorite restaurant. When I say we both were grubbing, we were grubbing. The whole table was covered with food. There was not any room for our drinks; that is how much food we had. I remember that day just like it was yesterday. That was our last brother and sister date we had together.

As the years passed on, Demetrius' and my relationship began to go downhill. Dee had a lot of issues going on, and he allowed those issues to have control over those he was once close to. We would text each other and converse with each other on social media occasionally, but it was not like how it used to be. I would pray for my brother and keep him covered at all times. Although I was his little sister, I was his second mama too. The loss of my brother was the hardest and most painful thing I have ever experienced in my life. I would not wish this on anyone. However, the loss of my brother has allowed life to gain so much. Even in my brother's death, I have seen God work in the lives of people who were connected to Dee and those that knew him, but not on a personal level. So many lives have been saved. So many people have learned how to forgive those that did them wrong. I could go on and on about how God has shown Himself.

I'm thankful for the 19 years God allowed Dee to be my brother. I miss and think of him daily, but I know that he is in a better place and that one day I will see him again.

Sincerely yours,
Your little Sister
Alexus

Tribute #2

For 36 years we shared life with each other, whether it was good or bad. We shared a lot more

good times than bad. From us both getting on each other's nerves to us not having enough hours in the day to spend with each other. I believe you're the only person to grow from a child to an adult and be scared to have fish with bones in it. But you loved seafood. Nephew you are truly missed, from the arguments to the laughs. Rest peacefully Nephew, Unc loves you forever!
#EVENINTHIS

Uncle PaPa

Tribute #3

Tribute to Demetrius Everett

Demetrius and I had a friendship that started in the barber shop. As we got to know each other better, Jesus was very much always the center of our conversations. He would come to the shop needing a haircut, but we would part ways having gotten so much more. The Lord knows what we need in our times of weakness as well in our times of strength. So, the Lord would always work it out so we could be alone in the shop, which allowed us to get spiritually naked with each other. Through our interactions with each other over the years, we learned a lot from each other and about each other.

One of the things I learned from our coming together was that it is okay for us as men to be open and honest with each other about our struggles. We would talk about those things that had us bound, and we would leave each other encouraged in the Lord. I really believe that is the part of our friendship that will be missed the most. All men should have one or two brothers they can be transparent with in times of need. It is a must in order for us as men to be successful in this world today.

Your presence has truly been missed, and I am a better man because of the friendship that we had. My hope is that all of the lives that you influenced will continue to grow and be cultivated. Dee, my prayer is to see you in glory someday.

God Bless!

Dwight Flowers

Tribute #4

In Loving Memory of Demetrius Everett

TO GOD BE THE GLORY!!!

I am so honored and thankful to have this opportunity to say what I'm really feeling. This is so hard. Who would have ever thought that I would be writing a tribute to you, and you're not here to share it with me. I'm really having a hard time typing this out, especially without my eyes tearing up and tears falling. I miss you so much. I LOVE YOU, and I always will.

When I first met you, it was like I had known you all of my life. You were and still are my little brother. I loved the way that you always expressed your feelings no matter if it hurt or not, but it was the truth, and I thank you for that. You were such an inspiration to everyone that you met. I never knew a young man so young as yourself that knew the Bible the way you did. Just that alone was awesome. You could and would quote that Bible word for word, and I was so amazed because you knew exactly what you were saying. Seeing you that way made me know that you were raised up in a spiritual environment, and to that I say "Thank you" to your family.

There's not a day that goes by that I don't think of you, wishing that you were still here, but I know that it would be very selfish of me wanting you to stay here on this earth knowing that we are going through all of these trials and tribulations. I know that you are in Heaven just having a joyous time.

I often sit back and laugh or smile remembering the things that we did together, and all I can say is "DD". Even when you didn't feel your best, you always put a smile on my face. DD, I can't and never will forget you, because you are not a person that is easy to forget. I LOVE YOU with all my heart, and there will always be a spot in my heart just for you. Continue to REST IN PEACE my friend, my brother, my buddy.

LOVING YOU ALWAYS,
Roxie Wheeler Parker

Tribute #5

"Ball, Ball", I really do miss you so much. I called you my "Ball, Ball" because you were fat and chubby when you were born. Not a day goes by that I don't think about you. You kept me company, we fussed and then made up, and we laughed. I miss you from just calling me for nothing. I miss you from asking me to pick the bones out of your fish. I miss you from laying on my bed like you were a baby. I miss calling you and telling you to get me a newspaper. I just miss you from walking and eating all times of the day and night. You could really eat too! "Ball, Ball" we all miss you! There is so much I could write, but it's really hard just thinking about you not being here. I never thought you'd leave us behind, but God always knows best. Continue to rest peacefully! Still love and miss you!

Love you,
Granny "Ma Mae"

Tribute #6

As I am trying to put my words and thoughts into this tribute, I can truly say that this is the hardest thing I've ever had to endure in my life, but God has graced me to go through it. Writing this book and even this special tribute is part of my healing process.

Every day, I think about you. I think about how chubby you were at birth. I think about how you made people laugh. I think about how you could eat and eat and never gain weight. I think

SPECIAL TRIBUTES

about how we used to hang out at the restaurants, parks, and malls. I think about how you protected me. I think about how you loved your sister, Alexus. I think about how you helped me with her. I think about how you loved to help others. I think about how you loved your Aunt Jet, Brittany, and Kendall. I think about how you used to turn flips and do cartwheels. I think about how you gave the teachers a "fit." I think about how you could be selfish and even stubborn at times. I think about all the ways you blessed my life. I think about your life and mine, both the good and the not so good times.

Even now, I'm thinking about how much you were really loved by so many. I miss you so much Dee. Most of all, I think about how you loved and praised the Lord, even till the Lord called you home. I prayed and believed God for your healing, but His will was done. God had a greater need for you and day by day, I understand it better.

You were an awesome man of God. I saw how God used you to minister to others. You had a BIG heart towards people. When you gave backpacks and school supplies to children in need, it really blessed my heart. You got that big heart from your Mommy!

There's not a day gone by that you're not on my mind. I've found myself texting your old phone number until one day I received a reply. I apologized to the person and told them why I had texted, and they told me that they would keep me in prayer. When I go past your old job, I think about how you used to turn those curves with that truck. Man, you would be leaning…lol.

I wish I could hug you one more time. I remember the last hug you gave me. It was so strong, loving, and warm. Mannn, I miss you! I try my best to stay strong for Alexus and the family, but sometimes I must allow and need God to help me. So, I have my moments of missing you, and then I regroup and move on because I know that one day I will see you again. I have peace knowing that you had accepted Jesus as your Lord and Savior. I have peace knowing also that you're not in pain, no more suffering, and no more struggles. I know that you are with the Lord. I know you would want your family to be strong knowing that you are at peace with the Lord. So, with all that I've written, I choose to serve God with my whole heart, mind, body, and soul so that I can see you again. Missing and loving you still Dee!!!

MOM

Tribute #7

I met DeeDee a few years ago on his birthday through Reese. DeeDee and I instantly clicked, which he also did with a lot of other folks. With me knowing DeeDee only a short period of time, he started calling me his nephew and I would call him Unk in return. Over the time, DeeDee and I became close. We became so close that people started actually thinking that we were really uncle and nephew.

DeeDee got me a job at Hess gas station while he was working there. That's when we really saw how much we had in common. We would sit there and joke all day about everything and on everyone. DeeDee was a very rare individual. He could've lit up the darkest room with his great personality, and he would've given someone the shirt off of his back without thinking twice or speaking on it later in the near future.

Long Live Three Five Seven

Aaron Moore

Tribute #8

I pray that this Facebook page remains. Although I would understand if it becomes too much for Demetrius Everett's family, please know that this young man touched so many lives, even an older woman like me. I love the fact that I can visit his page and be encouraged. His Christian insight blew me away, especially when his daily posts spoke to my then current situation.

I never got the gift of meeting him personally, but I am so happy that we became Facebook friends (although I can't seem to recall the particulars).

To Demetrius Everett's Mom: Thank you for bringing into the world and raising such an awesome young man. You did such a great job that God decided, in His infinite wisdom, to elevate him to angel status. God Bless you and your family.

Fidelia Rodriguez

Tribute #9

Demetrius Everett was an absolute smart and phenomenal young man. I was always amazed by his wisdom and intellect. I met him through his mom, Pastor Teresa Horne. He was always very respectful and always was full of humor. Demetrius had great potential and was full of fun and life.

I will always remember our first conversation where he trusted me enough, without knowing me, to share his heart. I could tell his mother had been praying and covering him in prayer. He oftentimes talked about the love he had for his family in our conversations. His presence will greatly be missed in the earth realm. He was the epitome of life and made up his mind to live his life to its fullest.

His knowledge of the Bible and his love for the Lord gave him great peace, and he has earned a great reward in heaven according to the Scriptures. I missed seeing his humorous posts on social media and his serious posts. He could always make me laugh when I would read his social media posts. He has made the transition into the presence of the Lord.

SPECIAL TRIBUTES

The Bible declares in 2 Corinthians 5:1, *"For we know that if our earthly house of this tabernacle were dissolved, we have a building of God, a house not made with hands, eternal in the heavens."*

I believe through his faith in God, that he now has a house not made with hands in the heavens.

Apostle Matthew Tillery

ABOUT THE AUTHOR

Evangelist Teresa Everett Horne, a native of Tarboro, North Carolina, is the wife of Pastor Gregory T. Horne and the mother of two adult children; Alexus and Greg Jr. She is the daughter of Rosa Everett Smith and Samuel Lee Lyons.

Evangelist Horne is an Ordained Evangelist of the Lord Jesus Christ, who carries a prophetic anointing upon her evangelistic mandate, preaching the Gospel of the Kingdom of God.

Evangelist Horne is a God-fearing woman who loves the Lord and His people and has a "soul winning" anointing upon her life.

She is an encourager, supporter of others, prayer warrior, and intercessor. Although she has endured much suffering in her lifetime, through it all she continues to stand on the promises of Almighty

God, and she steadfastly declares daily that ***#EvenInThis***, God gets all the Glory!

ORDER INFORMATION

You can order additional copies of Even In This, by emailing the author directly using the email address below.

Teresa Everett Horne

Email Address:

divinepurpose08@yahoo.com

Books are available at Amazon.com, BN.com and other online booksellers. Also, request copies at your local bookstore.

Please leave a review for this book on Amazon and let other readers know how much you enjoyed reading it.

Thank you!

www.ingramcontent.com/pod-product-compliance
Lightning Source LLC
Chambersburg PA
CBHW071157090426
42736CB00012B/2356